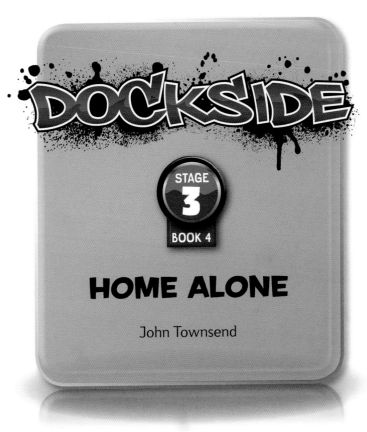

DOCKSIDE

STAGE
3
BOOK 4

HOME ALONE

John Townsend

Riverside Primary School

Janeway Street
SE16 4PS
Telephone 020 7237 3227 • Facsimile 020 7237 0047

RISING ★ STARS

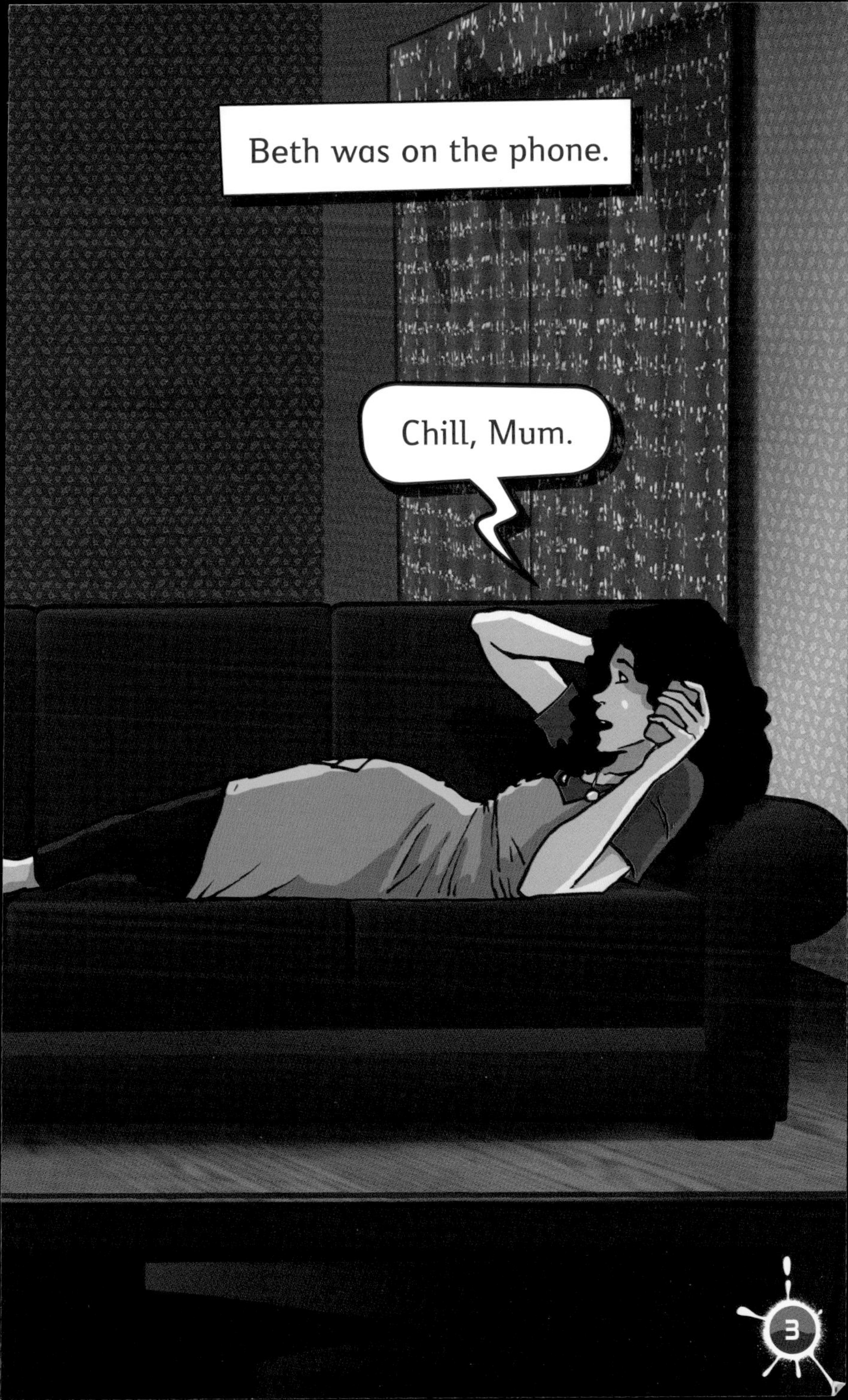
Beth was on the phone.
Chill, Mum.

Mum asked Taz next. He lay on his bed.

Mum was upset. "If your dad has been here, I'll go mad. He comes here and goes when I get home. Is that it?"

"You must think I'm slow. I can tell he's been here, you know," said Mum.